TRANSCENDENCE

Aremu Adams Adebisi

TRANSCENDENCE

(poetry)

Aremu Adams Adebisi

Copyright ©2018 Aremu Adams Adebisi

ISBN: 978-978-964-188-8

All rights reserved.
No part of this book may be reproduced, distributed, stored in a retrieval system or transmitted, in any form or by any means, electronic, electrostatic, magnetic tape, mechanical, photocopying, recording or otherwise without prior written permission from the Publisher.
For information about permission to reproduce selections from this book, write to info@wrr.ng
National Library of Nigeria Cataloguing-in-Publication Data

Printed and Published in Nigeria by:
Words Rhymes & Rhythm Limited
Suite C309, Global Plaza Plot 366, Obafemi Awolowo Way, Jabi District, Abuja, Nigeria.
08169027757, 08060109295
www.wrr.ng

CONTENTS

DEDICATION 7
Imageries 8
Timelessness 10
What Poetry Makes Of You 12
Little Black Child 14
Exceptions 16
Yaomu-l-Hisaab 19
Seven 22
Song Of A Mad Woman 23
Arrival Of The Rain 25
The Night Does Not Have To Sleep 27
Poet of a layman 29
Speak To Me 31
A Perched Bird Hears Words 33
Cacophonies 34
Alake 35
25 Hours, 61 Seconds: 37
Home 39
A Mortal In Me 41
Ellipsis 43
August Elegy 45
Ode To Death 46
For She Who Has My Youth 47

The Requiem 48
Book and Love 49
Dual Origin 51
Sweating In The Rain 52
A Poet And A Painter 54
Ballad Of The Sixteen Friends 55
uʍop əpᴉsdn 57
Definition Of A Poem 58
IN A SINGLE ROOM OF A WEST-AFRICAN .. 60
How You Unwind 62
Bliss At Sundown 65
silhouettes 67
Clothing 68
Tale Of Two Birds 71
Epitaph 73
Words And Bullets 74
A Love Poem 75
Aremu 77
Incoherence 79
Schadenfreude 80

DEDICATION

To dawn and sunset
before my eyes:

Hanreef, Sobuurah,
to Princess Karys M Richard;
Monsieur Poirson, Baba Ola Anobi,
to Mrs Memunat Adebisi

IMAGERIES

We begin poetry
by telling you to run away from your skin
because your skin is too tight for your body
and your body is a punctured mesh.
We tell you to burn, to burst into flames
and crave light in the glints of darkness
for it takes days to recognise the nights.
We ask you to shred your shadows apart
and make them fall behind you, doused in salts,
enwrapped in the silky smudge of clouds.
We embalm your bones; let them resonate
your flesh from within so you can be healed
in poetry — in the ambiguity of simplicity.
Sometimes we begin with words inarticulate,
with broken letters seeking paths in your thoughts.
We tell you 'God is dead...' (with an ellipsis)
and watch you grind books in-between your teeth.
We make letters stutter like memories,
while you draw reliefs from fleeting whole.
There are patterns and components in poetry
intertwined into your passion and emotions;
how one triggers another in few words.
And how do we assess how these make you cry?
We begin by saying a child died at birth by
our ruling

and watch the words register a home in your mind
for this is the child that made you clutch your breasts,
that made you grieve in tears pelted with iron.
We must consider healing you with an addendum
if we need to see you smile again;
so we write your child to be the star that glows
that you may find yourself watching behind a window.
How we begin is how we hold you to ransom,
how we provoke the greenlight of your heart,
how we make you dead and have you buried in ink.
There are things we never say in poetry
when in fact it seems they are being said;
like birdsongs, like echoes of sea-waters,
like a mother outlining his son's face from the dust.
Thus we must subtly begin poetry
by telling you how it never begins
and how it truly seems to have no end,
even as it paints yours in imageries.

TIMELESSNESS

The wind has me drifted
from across the curtained deep,
I touch shadows of birdsongs,
feel the tang of ash & dust on their beaks.

They smell like carnage,
carcasses of living men;
time denuded, but timelessness;
history retreats into a puddle of claret—

iron and bullets, rust and rose;
fate stutters in verdicts, I uninterrupt.

I smoke mud into a castle-kingdom,
full of chests and treasures—
a homespun, a worn-out tissue,
a ribcage of shredded tendon;

chatters of paupers in a wind din,
bones creaking in their throats.

Flutters of insects, I startle in black—
flight reminds me of descents, and
shipwrecks and crashes of airplanes...

and windowless homes made of salt.

Life unfolds at my bended knees,
I purify with speed and conviction

Trancendence

and memories — a gaudy butter-
fly, clasped in black and white.

I tread the length and breadth
of the vulture's wingspan,
of roared letters of seawaves...

I meander through eyes of eagles.

I sprawl mysteries, my brain shrinks;
the stars recognise me in the dark—
I seem to lug the self to the old
whilst decades pray me.

WHAT POETRY MAKES OF YOU

At such proximity he still can't see
    the bridge below his acute eyes,
        a white hulking shadow, a
silhouette
           serenading across the
moonbeams.

He lights a saturated wick,
    how candleless, lampless;
        holds onto it like breath, a clench
           of teeth, of fists defying
weakness—

they gaze all back, lines and rhythms,
    clogs and blocks, as if paying odes
        to interruptions — water in a
lidless
           kettle boils and boils
and boils.

Write a poem under your seawater,
    cover yourself in seaweeds,
        scrawl the language of sea
alphabets
           on waterbabies and
water-fairies.

Silence, a smoke of winds, a dream
    seeming in yellow wilts,

Trancendence

cacophonies,
          dusk and dawn riled in ink
stains:
             this is what poetry makes
of you.

LITTLE BLACK CHILD

I met a little black child on the road,
I met a little black child in the forest.

I met a little black child and thus I said,
'Little black child, why are you so forlorn?
Why are you so gazed like a glass?
You walk without shadows for the sun
does not find you a worth to shine on
nor to catch a reflection of her lucence.
The earth you bare does not recognise your feet,
and you have succeeded in making men purify
their bodies with pace at your beholding.'

She teethed and stoned me a trailed look
with her dust-filled eyes, her rust-filled eyes,
glowing in the requiem of a buried bone.
Her hair was tousled and her shroud stained
with blood dripping from between her loins.
Her face, outlined with incessant tears,
was covered with ash and countenance.

She heaved as if to answer my question,
as if to correct the perception of a living man.

Instead it was silence. Wind in her tongue.
Her breath smelt of war; men and children
sacrificed for the study of raucous guns.

Trancendence

She heaved again — a second time,
and the breath came to me like carnage,

like women raped into their bones
till their marrows gave way for threnodies.

Her silent heaving seemed different now;
she heaved and I could read them like books,
like an astrologist reading the fallen stars,
and I wondered about myself, my speech
seeming to her like a gust of wind.

'Little black child...', she hushed, silently,
her darkened face transitioning into beams,
and her arms thrown around my emptiness.
I heard her silence wreathe me with flowers
as her tempest motioned me to my grave.

EXCEPTIONS

(After Rick Barot's Ode To Interruption)

A boy leaves a gathering with a crumpled
face.
A boy is alienated from the school's
playground

because he adorns himself with a homespun.
He picks some pebbles and pelts them with.

A boy has his head rested on a limbed tree;
he is
sobering and smoking the wind at the same
time.

A boy mixes colours: red, yellow, green— a
gray
boy. A gray boy with eyes like fragment blue

and a sprawled body. You seat your gaiety
in a quiet room, watch your silent heart
empty

into a gulch of nettles. You are a moor, lost
in the ruins of childhood bonds and blood
ties.

A boy is walking and singing all to himself,
a different boy for each singing, with stalked

shadows aligning with each gait. A boy pours
himself into a sea. A boy is poured into a sea

and a requiem passes — our Lord, our
father,
we have cast the burden; let there be bloom.

A boy is writing a letter under a poor light,
on a shrinking skin. In a bedroom, upstairs

a boy holds a discarded dream with tweezers
and adds it to his collection. We all are
staring

straight into the flames we huddle around,
but
you — you look sideways, sitting miles apart

like a plague. A boy runs his fingers on scars
stitched across his face. Under a bridge, a
boy

counts the different cars running. Another
boy
for a minute. A boy goes through a family
album,

wonders how he is the only one left on each
page.
The same album he has been seeing for ages.

A boy is at the peak of a mountain, his head

seems thrown out, thinking of dimly warmth.

Sometimes, poetry never appears to us as figments
until we glean exceptions into thoughtful whole.

Trancendence

YAOMU-L-HISAAB

When people mention the word 'Terrorist',
I put it in a quotation mark, like the one above,
because what they usually mean are Muslim
men and women who strap bombs to bodies.

So it is my culture to strain my eyes
for names like Abdullah, Mohammed, Youssef,
when death tolls again in Maiduguri
or in Vatican City where the Pope lives,
with humans separated from their skins.

My little daughter will come back home
from school and when it is time for solat,
she will purify her body, wrist to elbow,
head to toe, and recite some Quranic verses.

I taught her Surat-ul-Ihsaan, where Allah
talks about humans and how they were formed.
Each human formed in the same way as others.

Last night, someone called the prophet a paedophile
on Facebook and I had blocked him before I could

think 'each human formed in the same way as others'.
My daughter won't be too amazed to hear this.

Patiently, I search for the coming of Isa when
the Muezzin calls to prayers in his guttural voice.
My cousin tells me about a man she wishes to marry
at nineteen. His voice is like that of the Muezzin.
I want to say it is too early when I remember girls
who have willed me their bodies at seventeen.

My little daughter is urging me for an excursion.
I don't know how to tell her the times are wrong
especially for a girl like her wearing hijab.
I don't know how to tell her there was a protest,
a worldwide protest for the eradication of Islaam.

Sometimes I want to say 'Peace', but the words
that come out from my mouth is 'Yaomu-l-Hisaab'.

Trancendence

When I touch the Qur'aan after I have urinated,
and I have not cleansed my body, 'Yaomu-l-Hisaab'!
When they say Allah's name is inscribed on woods,
on mountains, on the unpurified body of a new child,
Yaomu-l-Hisaab! When a Muslim brother says my being
a Muslim is not enough for me to make paradise,
Yaomu-l-Hisaab! I have no beards, Yaomu-l-Hisaab!
My trouser is not cut too low? Yaomu-l-Hisaab!

SEVEN

Let my days be filled with seven,
Seven wonders of the world;
And my life with seven heavens
And with bliss that seems unfurled.

Seven shades of radiant rainbows,
Let my seven sacraments
Cut across the seven rivers
And the seven continents.

Let me probe the seven mountains
and the seven seas.
Let me through the seven planets,
and the seven Pleiades.

Let me not in brunts of Hades,
And the brunt of seventh hell.
Let my seven sins be pardoned
And my seven days as well.

Play my world a note of seven:
Do. Re. Mi. Fa. So. La. Ti.
Find me peace, all seven Chakras
and in seven poetry.

SONG OF A MAD WOMAN

Your home is draped with fallen leaves,
Your shrine with delight from the ruins.
Your path is adorned with twisted twigs
And glorious flowers from every wilt.

I have folded your drenched apparels,
And collected the rainwater in a sieve.
When you come, you will drink and swim,
Stretch in the fullness of your phantom,
You whose cloth complements the sky.

When you come, we will talk at length
In the language of birdsongs. Your polished
Smiles, long dark, chalked face, bowing
In silence at my feet. My whetstone,
My bright onyx, revel in
Arrival of the stars
And come in dark shrouds visible to me.

Here you are, owner of my heart,
Come in and feel my dignity.
Let me wipe off the rain from your eyes
And the remnant dust from your brow.
Here, a seat in the clouds; sit and feed.
Your place is among the lofty ones.

Let us talk wildly about tales beyond,
And the mystery of laughter and delusion.
Watch me disrobe myself in your eyes

That people of the world may wonder
What a mad woman offers the wind
While here is your towering sunset
Relishing her lady with pure bliss and joy.

ARRIVAL OF THE RAIN

The rain has come again in crystal liquid
drops;
There is fullness in the seas, and on the
fields
The meadows revel in the splendour of
greenness.
And above our heads, beyond the stifling
roofing
Is a singsong splatter singing sleep-songs
And lush lullabies for our dreary eyes.

We should sleep in heaviness until
protuberance,
Until the dam has begun daring the sky's
clouds,
For the rain has come again in crystal liquid
drops
And the children are beaten beyond
excitements;
While the land becomes a tacky mud for
feeds,
The head is a talking-drum without flailing
strands.

How do we tell the tale that has to bear its
fang
That tomorrow is etched on the fronds of
yesterday
And that travellers crawl onto their paths to

fetch
The good guiding stars from the eyes of the moon.
And when tears mingle with heartbeats, we'd ask;
Hasn't the rain come again in crystal liquid drops?

THE NIGHT DOES NOT HAVE TO SLEEP

I see a night dressed in the finest regalia,
Mounted on a white horse adorned with bracelets;
Yet he sobers at the quick pace of every gallop
When though he should control this, he can; but why?
He says: one certain day has the rein to his horse.

I see a night chewing pleas in the shrine of gospels;
His wife is barren likewise his dear children
Suffer from the chronicity of evils and measles.
Where is Ifa? Where is Sanponna? Won't you pray to them?
He says: one certain day burns his tongue to the gods.

I see a night clothing the glints of lunar rays;
He sits, hurling stars against the earth surface
And would praise his brain by feeding his belly.
Why must you 'night' the 'already-nightly' night again?
He says: one certain day will gleam the darks after all.

I see a night being stoned in the gathering of colours.
They say he looks black and just devoured a banana.
That he has arms and could jump from trees to trees;
Still, he twinkles stars and makes the moon to shine; but why?
He says: one certain day will be tired and will need to rest.

Whatever happened to having sleepless nights!

POET OF A LAYMAN

"Great bard,
what do we do about the letters to my Romeo
in a faraway kingdom, over seas and
mountains?"

'I have cleared the lands for you, ma'am,
by planting your needs in their gardens.
I have also uprooted the weeds
so to make your seeds raw in the mouth
of that you intended for their devouring.'

"Oho! I see...
How toxic palm-wine can be!
It has made the gardener lazy and then, the
gardener has burdened on you his work.
Your lettered quills and slates will bear me
witness,
I will sack him before dawn!"

'Ma'am, I mean the allegories you asked
me to symbolise with romantic vignettes,
well flourished with rhetorics, paving way
for similes and dynamic metaphors in the
synecdochic mind of this faraway allusion.

"Hmm, I should get you, great bard?
Still, I beg of you to steady your tongue;
It seems going and coming in a way
that I can't hold onto their meanings,

making me ignorant of the executed."

'Pardon me, ma'am, I am a poet.
In case you start asking what that means;
I am the kind that separates your wardrobes
and then buries some under foamy lotions,
and then makes them dry, before ironing.'

"Praa!
Leave the laundry-work for the laundry-man,
what's your work if not to write me letters?'

SPEAK TO ME

Speak to me, child of life;
Speak to me in your battered soul,
Pummelled like a drunkard's housewife.

Speak to me, young lady,
holding my hands in your tiny palms
Which have been ground into fine pieces,
So weak and small for all their tenderness;
A hand that says more about life –
Of life impudence and brutality.

Speak to me, my dear;
Speak to me in your shaking voice
That holds traces of unseen sadness.
Tell me of battles life won against you
And how it raped your soul to bone.
Tell me young lady as I promise to tell no one.

Speak to me, will you?
Speak to my soul as a sister would.
Open my eyes to the thorny hands of life.
Were you not orphaned at the age of three?
Were you not raped three times a day?
Let the blast swim off in tears; tell me your past.

Where are you, child of life?
Can you speak to me this last time?

Why your carcass lies carelessly?
You left your word to me, why not your soul to God?
Why did you pierce your past in blast
When your blast war will soon be past?

Speak to me, I hear you not.
My speech wobbles in the silence of the wind;
Are you now the free-flowing breeze?
My words shatter upon the lightness of the sea;
Are you the moving current waves?
Finally, you are hunted into exile by life.

A PERCHED BIRD HEARS WORDS

A bird that holds the sky to ransom,
makes its wings twice as swift as air
on the back of the coursing wind;
it beholds itself in tolling space
and soars in endless clouds.

But a bird that perches on the roof,
clatters its feet on the rusty sheet,
her eyes well seated in perspectives,
her swinging tail in emptiness,
so it picks the words and sings:

'Guinea-corns in barrels, Akintunde
feed my mouth with worms. Journey
from the world beyond, feed my mouth
with worms. With sweet sweet worms,
Akintunde, feed my mouth with worms.
A bird does not perch without hearing
words.'

CACOPHONIES

Cacophonies, I hear them,
not, to them I listen, I listen
eagerly not, they shred, shred,
my ears, my shredded ears,
not, my auditory; cacophonies
in silent, silent fall of leaves,
breaths of empty tombs;
and I, hear them, thud, thud,
and mute, till, they talk, balk,
lips-sealed, wind, unblowing,
and I, not, listen, and I, not- I hear!

Trancendence

ALAKE

Beyond is drawn nearer to my breath,
It breathes deep in my vein,
I know what happens in the afterlife,
It is at the bridge of my nose;
Though blurry, but my eyes see them.

Who buries a grave in my eyes
And makes its spirit bleat at my feet;
Near the tray whence I pick the grains,
Near the teeth of my running mind,
Kneading griefs into a subtle plow?

I know the non-living take the form of the living
And that is where they call the afterlife,
But how do I live in the afterlife when I'm not dead?
Where do the living meet the dead?

They meet here:
In the wind that courses through the face,
In the intervals of soliloquy,
In the buffets of silence
Trailing the tails of heavy feet,
In the sudden sound in the ears
That rings and rings like a piped call.

Humans die only to live again,
Their spirits breathe as birds,

Some as plants, some as objects,
And some as souls that trouble a nightmare;
But Alake, what have you become
With two horns in a pile of grasses?

Trancendence

25 HOURS, 61 SECONDS:

When we sing an ode to interruptions, we find you
Fractured across time & place. We find you pucker
In fits of laughter, quadriplegic, matted in shadows.
Your mother picks flowers in the garden, you pick
nettles in moors. Your mother grabs a ring of afterglow
from the ether, her leathery hands are time souvenirs.
You explode from the guttural, your un-heartfelt voice
Blares into the atmosphere. We think about your past,
Drape their blemishes in ellipsis, your morrow is the
Parentheses of Fate. While your arms sprawl, we think
Of how to knit your fabrics. So we say 'breathe', but you
Un-breathe your existence and your body shrinks into
The evening of your thoughts. We live life anew. Skins
Anew. Feet treading trodden paths anew. I say, I am at

Where the flight of a bird is a precursor. Where silence
Is the passage of Jibreel. Where angels sniff the scent
On uncovered hair. Where daughters kneeling down to
Mothers is fetish & Gomorrah is bedding your woman.
I tell you many things, but what do you know? I tell you
Be sad, be sad when you write a poem or two. Let the
World know your mother dies in imageries while alive.
When you write about your father, make sure you period.
Forget he talks to you in dreams, forget he comes as
A bird. Forget Africa if you can hurry into the embrace
Of the shores. I tell you many things and how you evolve
In shining wilts, bones and bullets; but what do you know?

HOME

Brother, must I remind you?
Snakes do not eat termites again,
It is termites that now eat snakes;
Birds do not feed on worms again,
Worms now feed on birds mystically;
The lizards and the wall-geckos—
Those we tried to catch by the tails
Are now the fiends in our countenance.

Brother, please take us home.

This bond is scorched by the sun
And is thoroughly drenched by the rain
That when you walk to the market-place
You'll see it being shaggy and littering
In the mocks of the market-women.

This tie also has been severed by tongues—
The tongues of palmists and marabouts
That make distinct the day from the night
And your mirror which is my mirror
From my mirror which is your mirror.

So we lost a sense of belonging—
That sense of belonging
You sent salt because my mouth was stale
I sent rainbows because you felt stormy;
You sent an arsenal because of my brawl,
I sent hares for the gluttony of your lion;

For this home must be rooted by the four-walls
And its roofing must be well lidded.

But those are long past and gone
For this home is now falling and dilapidated;
It has cracks whose bricks passers-by use
As stones to break palm-kernel nuts and
Little children in the carpentry of their toys...
Brother, you should renovate!

How I wish I could do this,
But I am a juvenile and you are older.
I can only see while on my feet, dear elder.
You are the ashes when the fire dies,
You are the shelter of these heads,
So brother, please take us home.

A MORTAL IN ME

In the eclipse of his lucid world,
A mortal was seen
In my living lifeless body,
Wandering through the valleys of life
In a daring adventure.

He had colours like mine,
And in my favourite raiment
He danced with such abandon
To rhythm I merried to
Before being tamed by the hands of night.

Was it me? No, it can't be!

I don't know of rulers, yet the mortal in me
Claimed to shake the hands of a Pharisee.
I know not of crimes,
Yet he fought his ways to atrocities.

Hustling from thins to thorns,
Bustling from staid scenes to the obscene.
He smiled more to strangers,
Frowned upon my acquaintances.

His runs made my heart beat,
His gains found me a smile,
But his pains led to a wry cry
Which pierced through the parts of my soul,
As I came to the reality of my lifeless body.

Was it me? No, it can't be!

I glanced everywhere in search for answers:
The fan was singing with its three arms,
Hung pictures stared at my confused face,
The walls remained mute as they have been for ages,
Everywhere was silent.

Only the crickets could be heard
Chirping in their muddy floors,
Only the owls' whistles elevated
From a distant grassy wood.

Then I thought I heard a sound.
Yes, I heard a sound!
The beats of a thoroughly-used heart
Under a heavy perspiration of its exhaustive self.

Was it me? No, it can't be...

Trancendence

ELLIPSIS

Those who crawl back to seek
the earth from its depth, we greet you;
waters of the running deserts,
songs of farewells on eyelids,
echoes that name fears and shadows.

Those who forsake their features
to leave their eyes behind,
we greet you when you leave the earth,
we greet you when you return.
The pap-seller-of-heaven does not forget
you—
he fetches you your garment, you flit;
he fetches you your paraphernalia, you
concede.

We do not leave the hoe to them, we leave
the blade;
we do not leave the grasses, we leave the
roofing
water does not shed from our eyes —
we shed iron and bullets, we shed fertile
lands.

Those who now speak to the wind in secrets,
how do you make the leaves wave?
You are as near to us as our breath and
bones;
you stalk our silence to steal our pains.

How shall we name your absence?
We will build anew home from heated clay,
carve out of shining wood for adornments;
we will pay your visits to kinsmen
and feed your eyes with nectar.

There will be salt and honey and bean-cakes,
your garden tended to, your shrine
consulted,
for home you leave behind is as strong as
grief.
And when you come again as a bird
or as an abstract looking on from the din,
you will meet us well, you will be in peace
and greet us as a stranger we won't
recognise.

AUGUST ELEGY

My stars have gone dim
into the abyss of the night,
my tongue has been wrung of a voice;
I am a wood in the solitude of motion.
My flowers have wilted,
I tread on paths filled with yellow leaves
and rotten seeds attracting houseflies.
My days of youth are running back to me,
I can feel your pats on my back, your pecks
canoodling the petals in my cheeks, your voice
rising through the clouds, in the wind,
seeking me out from among the mammoth.
When peace is asleep, silence fills the void;
you are the song in the flute of an elegist.
The river mocks me for she has a source,
the trees mock me for they have roots,
houses mock me for they have roofings,
whom shall I mock, I who have no one;
I who have lost the beginning towards an end;
I whose days have lost the whim for a sun?
They say people die to be born again,
but I say you won't die, you won't die
for you will always be here in my heart
living your roaming dreams.

ODE TO DEATH

Heavy
wind
blows away
the fire, the logs
and the boiled water
in the steaming pot.

FOR SHE WHO HAS MY YOUTH

You hold me to ransom thus
With your elfin eye-lashes,
Eyes of the sea-shells,
Eyes of the naked treasure,
Eyes that dare crystal orbs
Found in the deepest parts of seas.
I will wait upon your door
Like a toddler lumping for honey,
And will keep knocking, now and then,
Like the water lapping at a shore.
Your heart turns prayers into realities.
Your smiles, like the sun of the eventide,
Most serene and anodyne upon my fret.
Daughter of the flames that do not burn,
Daughter of the pristine stream
That courses down the shrine of Oluweri.
A lover will sing a song in the woods
And I your lover, will sing another;
He will sing of candies and thatched huts,
I will sing of milk and grasses
For these are the source of his song;
He will sing of music and abattoirs,
I will sing of flutes and cattle
For these are the source of his song;
But when he will sing of his woman,
I will only sing of you.

THE REQUIEM

I write a poem for my love
It sounds like a god to me,
It leaps in bounds in my tongue
And makes me smile! smile!

I write a poem for my love
It reeks of a smoke to me,
It fumes into the sky of my eyes
And makes me cry! cry!

Who has seen where she orates
The one with the crown.
Who has seen where she whispers
The one with the thorns.

I speak of the sun to my love
She feels restless and listless,
Her voice stutters like a raindrop
As her conscience gives her away.

I speak of the moon to my love
She is so happy like the wind,
She courses upon my feelings
And plunders inside my groins.

Who has seen where she goes
The one who separates
The day from the night
So that the day is for him
While the night is for me.

BOOK AND LOVE

We started our love with prefaces
without a table where contentment
could be listed with priorities —
a table of contents.

We love in crystal leaves,
white as delight, transparent,
bound together with a hard cover —
the shell of our hearts.

We put love into action
in the chasms betwixt parallel lines
as she moans in sprawled alphabets
and in knotted contextual meanings.

We smile in acts and fight in sequels
to be seen as the cast in scenes
at the end of every chapter.

As each page flips and drags
till the antagonist is the protagonist
and the latter soon is the former,
we take the climax for a coin;
a head or a tail —
a comedy or a tragedy.

And when it ends with a tail
we'd see it to be a drama
written by our hearts

with a beginning
and an end.

DUAL ORIGIN

Lady, my heart
does not hold any love for you;
It has died with the rain
Days of holding you close to my heart,
Like you were the very breath to it.
Days of sculpting your face in solitude,
Thinking when next they meet
They'd kiss and hold each other
For long into a boiling spring
Till wayward letters stray into realms
That gladden God's bewilderment.

How exhilarating!
Shredded thunder, hot sinful moon,
The girth which your legs spread,
Mounted- I, thrown across its cusps,
And I found rhythm in a stuck leash.
We were lost. I thought we were lost
When angels were stained with blood
And our eyes beheld in church silence,
And our hands, lurking in empty rooms.
Pray for me, lady— pray for me.
My heart did not hold any love
For you; it has died with the reign.

SWEATING IN THE RAIN

She says my poems are too indecent
and immoral, her woman left unadorned,
her rooms left unclosed with metaphors.
She says I do her a lot of injustice,
and woe betides my hands when no honour
they stain for her comparison with
jewelleries.
She says with a smile that I understand
too well, and throws her body upon me.

Should I not corrupt the world again
when her fragrance perfumes in nectars
and the stars adorned with radiance dare
her in nudity, beautiful, with breasts,
dark, full and round to beaded waist.
They overwhelm my hands still, when filled,
neither too big nor too small, with surface
harmonious and smooth for their surge
until a quiver shoots, war boils in my loins

and she wills me her body to live in.
Until I find shelter in pleasured temples,
watch her mute in ecstasy, her almond eyes
tattooing my body, fingers digging in my
skin.
We war to dawn till words break to paradise
and I, marauding into the depth of
sweetness.
Flamed dugout, a sweat in the rain, her

Trancendence

sultry
night infiltrated by the coarseness of my day.

Should I not corrupt the world again
when that discontent woman begs for more,
and I know how to tame the greediness.
When every orifice becomes a locked room
with keys thrown into the sea of wetness.
When I dare the thrills of her hill, lips
parted,
oil in-between, mouth arched into a birdsong,
and I hear my name surrounded by angels.

Soon, two bodies clatter, dipped in honey,
sugared in musk and saffron, with scents
like green leaves. Both will walk the moon
again
when the sun sets and wearied legs are
dewed
and hunger is poured into a stream of gold;
when torched by the wind of memories and
feelings spell bewilderment into the eyes of
God.

A POET AND A PAINTER

A painter lays his tools to paint,
I lay my tools to write.
He brings out his brush,
I bring out my quill.
He brings out his canvas,
I bring out my slate.
He talks of Titian and his Assunta,
I talk of Shakespeare and his Sonnets.
He says he has a palette of multiple colours,
I say I have thoughts of multiple shades.
He runs a colour into another
and says it is blending,
I run a thought into another
and say it is musing.
He sketches out a light paint,
calls it a blotwork.
I sketch out my fragmented thoughts,
call it a groundwork.
He runs his perspectives,
I run my imageries.
He paints fragments into whole
using his golden section,
I weave words into depth
using my rhetorics.
But when he paints a masterclass,
I have written of his painting
and him, the painter.

Trancendence

BALLAD OF THE SIXTEEN FRIENDS

Towards gold, towards gold,
  Towards gold onward.
Straight to the jungle of death
  Went the sixteen friends.
In search of gems, in search of pearls,
  In search of diamonds.
Straight to the jungle of death
  Went the sixteen friends.

Demons left, spirits right,
  Wild boars hard to girt.
Straight to the jungle of death
  Went the sixteen friends.
Their bullets off, their cutters pierced,
  Three friends badly hurt.
Straight to the jungle of death
  Went the thirteen friends.

Lions roared, tigers growled
  Foxes howling blood.
Straight to the jungle of death
  Went the thirteen friends.
Their hearts beat fast, their cold feet ran,
  Six friends got injured.
Straight to the jungle of death
  Went the seven friends.

Among the trees some monsters hid
  And pounced on them all.

Straight in the jungle of death
  died the seven friends.
Their carcasses vultures preyed on,
  While their bodies sprawled.
Back from the jungle of death
  None the sixteen friends.

Trancendence

Hang your poetry upside down
let them read with bended eyes.
drag their rightness to their wrongness
As their burden feels the skies.
bid your diction from its ending,
Crush the world's known stereotypes.
Write your feelings from their limits,
Wear on them your deviant stripes.
Where to, wherefore, whence and what is
poetry without its shades?
Write a line and make it struggle
In their eyes for accolades.

upside down

DEFINITION OF A POEM

We don't just write a letter, string some
letters into a word, some words or some
lines,
a group of words or lines, a long sentence
or another broken off into a clause, a phrase,
a syllabic sound, a morpheme or an
inexpressiveness
of what the mind intends, what the heart
beats
for in anticipation of meanings, signals
articulated in gestures, endeavours, under
the duress of pain, grief, bliss, memories,
erasures and incomprehension of life's
mystery,
and say we have not written a poem,
whereas
a poem is nothing and everything that
belongs
to poetry and with consideration for rhetorics
or inconsideration of them, and even of
patterns,
structures, components, adhering strictly to
rules
or not, overrun with punctuations and
without,
communicating a message, feelings or
leaving
one with gimp understanding of how the
mind works,

Trancendence

hidden or open, personal or shared, soft or congeal,
relatable or felt like the trails of birds in the sky,
explosive or not, inexplicably naming itself in forms,
themes, styles and titles with a concentration
or no concentration like the songs of birds, printed
or unprinted, submitted or kept, lost or found,
original, stolen or imitated from excesses,
inspired in dreams, by humans or nature, coherent
or not that one may know it is something that flows
from the beginning to the end in thirty lines or so,
something like this, without a full-stop, and still
be regarded a simple sentence of no definition...

Aremu Adams Adebisi

IN A SINGLE ROOM OF A WEST-AFRICAN

It begins with seven, u(n)sually:

Two on the bed, the crème de la crème.
Comfort comes from where the standing fan
blows, wearily fixed to work in monotone
and one-dimensionality.

They engage in a heated embrace
of two bodies finding each other a river,
dared to shore in ecstasy, spurred on
by the softness and fluffiness of their stead.

This bed is sacred, a treasure trove,
and no one is to sleep on while away.

There is one on the couch, the middle class,
who has learnt to face the Qiblah and keep
nightmares away, sleeping like a
mannequin.

She doesn't bother herself with what
happens
at the other end as she sleeps with her back
to it, and all her dreams and schemes
well tucked in the wave of indifference.

She enjoys the leaking air that comes from
where the fan blows, drools carelessly in it.

Trancendence

Four lie sprawled on a moth-infested mat,
ribs outlined with woven strands.
They reek of sweat and malnourishment,
each clapping into his ears heavily
to riddle the whinnies of mosquitoes.

These are the masses, the hoi polloi.

Now and again, a child learning how
to wet his dreams willingly, raises his head
to take a peep at his mother at all fours
and his father taking her from behind.

He is lost in the reality and touches himself
till his father's eyes find him in
bewilderment.

Tomorrow's morning, this child will be asked
what he saw last night and if he does not
say,
he may end up sleeping in bed as caution.

HOW YOU UNWIND

I live my life as I want not to live my life.
I have someone I love who has no one she loves.

At 25, I have attained everything a man craves for.
Name it: a good wife in memory, beautiful children

Inside my groin, and a house with no structure.
I am at present wearing my past shoes for the day.

I am wearing them very right—ly— wrong—ly—
The left for— the right, (for) the right— (for) the left.

Tie knotted straight— I look a perfect gentleman
With a crumpled string of laced fastening

Hanging down his neck. I rush out hurriedly
Slowly to catch the early bus with my briefcase

Tremendously handled. A school girl — or is it a boy

Of no gender— runs across like a gazelle.
Someone

Says s/he is running into the future in yesterday.
I do not disagree while I shake my head repeatedly.

I am inside the bus now as it motionlessly moves
Towards destinations that aren't our destinations.

But this strange man seated beside me I think I am
Very familiar with in all thoughtlessness. For as soon

As he covers his countenance with dark linings,
Then I know for sure he is no man but a vestige

That tries as much to look exactly as I am. Someone
Presses the bell now. A bus-stop is reached? Again,

Someone presses the bell now, and it tolls
Into the cries of a little child. And I wonder why

No one is coming down; why the driver is moving
So leisurely fast; why all gazes seem to stare at me

In quivers; why everything slips backwards from
The bell, the man, the schoolgirl, tie & shoes, to me.

BLISS AT SUNDOWN

these ones come in sunrise, dragging dawn
on their feet, little children of whom the sun
speaks, in lights and shimmering morns.
their white souls, crystal darkened eyes,
gaited shadows littering with every burst
of youth, and hearts filled with lecterns.

these ones are made in their father's house
with eyes like eagles, feet buried under dust.
when they come, they burst into flames
of din chasing the moon from its course,
till silence wearies me, age flogs my eyes,
the fleeting past tolling a bell in my head.

they will dance the dance of their fathers;
little ones who wave my skin to my face,
who speak in tongue that bares my filigrees.
their warring tender arms, intoxicating
taunts,
their twitching legs, how they meet and grab
and roll and throw. these ones will fetch me
a crown and a name beyond the seven seas.

oh day, be gone with your rash radiance;
let dusk pave me home, that my sweats
and sorrows may be dried in the beholding
of my little ones. that I may scoop the
toddling
in my hands; the two others daring the wind

towards me, i may plant on my waiting thighs.
that i may feel her lady woman my groins
and i search in her body a new lovely child.

SILHOUETTES

at the mouth of the graves
are tales you won't tell your heart
to uphold and not to forget,
as there are memories too difficult
to make even yesterday comprehend;
like songs heaping from mothers' tongues
like a child riding the back of the wind,
like sadness teaching laughter
how to sleep and never wake again...
before you learn how to swim
first learn how the river flows;
there is grief in the silence of the ageing
that begs for skies and wings.
my own silence is a figurine
i carve into it eyes and nostrils
to know what death would kill me,
and to see where shadows go
when the lights are off.

CLOTHING

Because my body is a country, a water confluence,
and a country is me and I am me with flesh and bones.
Because when we trace the marks on our faces and palms,
we find dust and ash in a rule of tussle between humans and jinns.
Because when I wear the Sari— either the Ghagra or the Pavada,
I let the Pallu drape over my shoulder freely, carelessly,
or tuck into my waist, stretching towns from Nepal to Tamil.
Because the Hanfu explores curves, tied with a Sash around the waist,
and the Kimono finds straight lines appealing, influenced by the Hanfu,
sharing an origin of drawings and designs—
two hands that applaud.
Because when I put on the Sherwani, with the Sarong patterned
around my waist and the Tembel Hat almost covering my face,
I find a wedding in Rajasthan, moving my feet to the Khmer dance,
with delicious Hummus and Falafel dancing down my throat.

Trancendence

Because the Keffiyeh holds two races in one,
a black and a white,
and the Jallabiyah, a long tunic garment,
says in purity is peace.
Because when I attempt to wear the Boubou,
the Pagne or the Danshiki,
I find myself ravened in tribes whose hearts
are as pure as honey,
skins like iron, and eyes as valiant and aging
as the eagle's span.
Because the Buckskins and the Poncho have
a long history
that cuts across the Andes people and the
Native Americans,
and the Huipils of the Tlapanec people is a
hundred panels in one.
Because when I wear the Sarafan with a
Beret and a Klomp on my feet,
I see myself a Matador at the Eiffel Tower,
overlooking the Red Square.
Because the Kilt, the Lederhosen and the
Smock-frock have me
reminiscing on great warriors of the past,
knowledgeable men
who once donned the wears for the
unification of humankind.
Because Gakti is of the Sami people who are
the people of reindeer
and the Tapa cloth can be used to decorate
walls and for poetry,
and also sing the Tonga, sip Fiji's Kava drink
and the Samoan Vaifala.

Because clothes do not betray the thread, the yarn and the spindle
and do not negate the body when they cover its nakedness.
Because either good or worn-out, white or black, loose or fitting,
an apparel or a homespun, they are all made from animal skin.

TALE OF TWO BIRDS

The liberal bird has swum the sky
And has breathed new every breath,
Above the sky riding the wind,
Known as a free flying birth.
The liberal bird would sing of gain.

The hindered bird was meant to sing
Songs of its new passing set,
Within its soul that looked the sky,
As was confined down to earth.
The hindered bird would sing of pain.

The liberal bird would laugh in pride
To every little insect pecked.
And would battle in courage
As older flying birds were checked.
The liberal bird would sing of feeds.

The hindered bird was let to eat
Dirty crumbs that fell to ditch.
Made to battle none other
Than its sorry battered wish.
The hindered bird would sing of needs.

The liberal bird would sing to God
Swaying tail to envied pitch.
It dipped its wings in the sunrays,
As it made the sky its niche.
The liberal bird would sing of range.

The hindered bird was not to sing
In fine tunes of noble breeze.
Hoarsely singing to heaven,
Freedom, freedom, freedom pleas.
The hindered bird would sing of change.

These two won't be alone in sight
If they know the might of day and night.
And this I hope someday to see.
And this I hope someday to see.

EPITAPH

Write a dirge upon my gravestone
That I was without a name.
All I wrote were rhymes and rhythms
And none seemed a heart to claim.
All I wrote were mere assumptions
That I'd live without an end.
All I used were verbose dictions
That none wished to comprehend.
How I spelt the world umop apisdn
How I spelt peotry wrong;
Show my days my scarlet writings
Pull their sunset lines along.

WORDS AND BULLETS

Tell the world that I am broken
into hundred slanted rhymes,
though I know I am connected
with the quest for paradigms.
Tell my lover she's forgotten
in the ruins of yesterday,
tell my morrow he is rusty
and his days are castaway.
Let me be the lonely piper
piping down the valleys wide,
let my mother know she's waiting
for a son without a pride.
Let the thousands who expect me
know my death is thoroughbred.
I am here with words and bullets,
I am painting Fate in red.

A LOVE POEM

    When we are in love, we do not whisper,
we do not talk too much, we forget poetry
    easily and all it represents in imageries.
We watch an elocutionist stutter in utter
    shock. We see a bird sitting on an olive tree
look beyond the grove, look beyond the road,
    far into the sea and we stare into the sea
and find deserts in waters. No seawaves
    slapping at the shore, no boats, no sailors,
no mullet smoked on a wood oven, no child
    building a sand-castle. We wonder why this is
only to see a rice field blighted with diseases,
    a child in Maiduguri whorled in shackles
because he is found at the European shore,
    running away from war, away from shadows.
Why, Beloved, say I do not love you as you want
    but I have sworn upon my mother's frets
that I do. For what better way I will say you
    remind me of poems unwritten, books I wish
to leaf through unopened and words
    at their silence? What better way to say
each time I think of your bed, I am gripped by

    the hands of a little boy with eyes plucked
out by scavengers? Let the sun set and I will
    smoothen your back with musk and saffron,
grab your waist, send chills down your spine.
    But I see them still, eating into my sleep,
seated in my eyes— young boys from Aleppo,
    old men in Afghanistan spared by bullets.
I love you, Beloved— Amen. Till death do us part.

AREMU

(the first male child)

Birthed in the factory of nothingness
Where none is deemed a birthright,
The foetus that precedes residuals
Towards the world of men...

I, Aremu, share my name
With Orisha-nla.

The clothes I have worn are
In my receptacle, waiting
To be worn upon the rest.
I suck sagged my mother's breasts
Leave their clutches for the next.

For so when the calls are made
And the ears do not fail to heed,
The titles fall at my favour
As my parents relish in answering.

I am that apex seed aside
In abodes of fertility,
And that which the barren seek
To have their troubles shared.

The land I come from is
Often larger than normal
And my milking feeds would

Be full like the brightest of moons.

When the marks become stretched
And the body could not help but own,
You would know I, Aremu,
Have trodden the path of birth.

INCOHERENCE

I aks
  a brid
     waht ti
        snigs

adn ti
  rpelsie
    in wrods,
      bdoy

adn s-
  uol of
    wihc si
      peotyr.

SCHADENFREUDE

Here I am slipping, here you are sleeping
beside me, refrigerating the sun rays,
with soft face transitioning into beams,
sculpted into chairs with long, wide, legs,
of broadsword, of ironclad, like the steeled
shoes of a horse gamboling inside your belly.
Here I prey, here you pray, and your words
stray into the eyes of God, and He sends
forth
for Mikhail among His angels, and you scoop
a feline with paws larger than a leopard's,
feed it with purrs from rainy mist and rats
gathered in body-bags, too shock to breathe.
Here I am dying, here you are dyeing, nose
twitched, eyes obscured into the remnants
of your morn. I watch you too closely as you
lower the fabrics into steaming tubs, moored
by diligence with spine arched by cold stone,
and hands fumbling with sweet afterglows.
Here while I write, here you say it's not
right,
and a cold wind like a razor scrape across
my face. And I am stung by nettles in the
imageries I stain, poetry in departures, I,
waved at with both hands. Song about the
moon falling fast into flames and memories.
Here does not feel like home, for I am at the
enemy's ground, for I live off on colours that
disagree with yours, for I wave black and I

wave beards and I wave a turban and I wave
God that mentions the contingency of bombs,
and I shoot, shoot a sparrow; and you shoot
shoot an empty nest? I am in chains because
a sparrow holds a breath and an empty nest.

AREMU ADAMS ADEBISI is a graduate of Islamic Studies and an Economics major at the University of Ilorin. Adebisi's works have been published on several platforms, including the WRR Poetry platform, Misty Mountain Review, Kalahari Review, AOIslamic and Africanwriters amongst others. He has also been published in anthologies like the *'Wind of Change'*, *'Love Poetry Anthology'* and *'The Train Stops At Sunset'*.

In 2015, Adebisi was listed among the top 50 poets who rocked Nigeria and he has clinched a number of runner-up positions in literary competitions, chief of which are the *Eriata Oribhabor Food Poetry Prize*, the *Talented* and multiple editions of the *Brigitte Poirson Poetry Contest* (BPPC). He edited the *Purple* Magazine and co-founded the Wordiators poetry movement.

SUMMARY

Transcendence basically is poetry at its dynamics, the sea of emotions and the bull-eye of mysticism. Its imaginary invasion is parallel to that of a landscape painting as it traces the different shapes and components of words that appeal to sensibility. It tackles life from a standpoint that oscillates between abstraction and anecdote in sections thoroughly layered and enjoyed. Tending to break into the unprecedented at each turn of a page, this collection of poetry certainly stalks its mystery.

www.ingramcontent.com/pod-product-compliance
Lightning Source LLC
Chambersburg PA
CBHW051349040426
42453CB00007B/480